Grasshoppers

Melvin and Gilda Berger

SCHOLASTIC INC.
New York Toronto London Auckland Sydney
Mexico City New Delhi Hong Kong Buenos Aires

Photographs: Cover: George D. Lepp/Photo Researchers; page 1: George D. Lepp/Photo Researchers; page 3: Myrleen Ferguson Cate/PhotoEdit; page 4: Gregory G. Dimijian/Photo Researchers; page 5: Jeff Lepore/Photo Researchers; page 6: George D. Lepp/Photo Researchers; page 7: Rod Williams/Bruce Coleman Inc.; page 8: Stephen Dalton/Photo Researchers; page 9: Stephen Dalton/Photo Researchers; page 10: Stephen Dalton/Photo Researchers; page 11: E.R. Degginger/Photo Researchers; page 12: Norman O. Tomalin/Bruce Coleman Inc.; page 13: Scott Camazine/Photo Researchers; page 14: R. Austing/Photo Researchers; page 15: Gary Retherford/Photo Researchers: page 16: John Serrao/Photo Researchers

ISBN 0-439-44540-X

12 11 10 9 8 7 6 5 4 3   2 3 4 5 6 7/0

Printed in the U.S.A.
First Scholastic printing, September 2002

Finding grasshoppers is fun.

Find the grasshopper
on a leaf.

Find the grasshopper
on the ground.

Grasshoppers are insects.

Fun Fact
Grasshoppers have two pairs of jaws and a few small teeth.

Most grasshoppers eat plants and seeds.

Grasshoppers hop.

Fun Fact
Grasshoppers have 4 short legs and 2 long, strong back legs.

Grasshoppers' back legs push them up into the air.

Fun Fact
Male grasshoppers chirp to find mates.

Grasshoppers sing.

They rub their wings together.

Fun Fact

Their huge eyes let grasshoppers see in all directions.

Grasshoppers have 2 big eyes.

Many grasshoppers also have
2 or 3 small eyes.

Female grasshoppers lay eggs.

Fun Fact

Baby grasshoppers are called nymphs.

The eggs hatch into baby grasshoppers.

Grasshoppers are hard to catch!